D1276853

The Brown Adobe Sampler

For a Taste of New Mexico

by Julienne V. Brown

illustrated by Karel Hayes

Copyright © 1988 by Julienne V. Brown and Karel Hayes
All rights reserved. No part of this book may be reproduced without the express written permission
of the author and illustrator.

Library of Congress Catalog Card Number: 88-72067

ISBN: 0-9621170-0-5

Published by THE BROWN ADOBE, INC.
Box S-245, St. Davids, PA 19087

*Should you have any questions, comments or suggestions about this book, or have difficulty in
obtaining any of the ingredients, please contact us at the above address.*

Printed in The United States of America by Indian Valley Printing, Ltd.
Second Printing 1990
Third Printing 1992

The text of this book is dedicated to John W. Brown, without whom I may never have been introduced to "The Land of Enchantment". And, to Daniel and Will, who share our love of New Mexico and its great food.

—J.B.

The illustrations in this book are dedicated to my husband, Brent Gorey, and our son, John, who shares my interest in art.

—K.H.

John

Great appreciation and thanks go to our many reviewers who spent hours testing and tasting these recipes. Ellen Barolak was especially helpful with editing and the publishing process.

Special thanks go to the greatest New Mexican cooks, my sisters-in-law, Amy Boule and Marian Schifani, both of Albuquerque, for all their input and assistance and for being, truly, our "New Mexican Connection" for all these years! Others from our New Mexico family, especially Carolyn and Gil Pryor and George Brown, have also contributed.

Table of Contents

On the road to Taos.

S. Francisco de Asís

Introduction

New Mexico is nicknamed "The Land of Enchantment"--and, indeed, it is! In New Mexico, the architecture is adobe (dried mud brick), and the sun always shines. In New Mexico, the American Indian culture mingles with Spanish, Mexican and Anglo influences to create a unique and exotic atmosphere. In New Mexico, mountains and mesa arise from the tumbleweed desert to reach for the magnificent sky. And, in New Mexico, great food is served.

Authentic New Mexican food is largely unknown to most in this nation. Only those who have had the good fortune to live or visit there know what they are missing. This food is quite different from that south of the border in Mexico, as well as from what is known as "Tex-Mex" or the dishes served in other states. It is the Pueblo Indian influence which has made this food unique.

Once accustomed to the wonderful flavors of New Mexico, it is difficult to do without them. This was the sacrifice we made when moving East years ago. Fortunately, family in Albuquerque and Pecos kept us in supply of the necessary ingredients to continue this indulgence. Sharing our meals with friends, we've learned that we are not alone in our love of New Mexican food. This great interest in the foods we've been serving guests, accompanied by requests of how to prepare them, led to THE BROWN ADOBE, Inc. Our company was started for the purpose of bringing real New Mexican food to places outside that state.

Included in this book is a sampling of some of the most popular and authentic dishes of New Mexico. All can be made as spicy hot or mild as you desire, and are easy to prepare. Totally unpretentious, New Mexican cooking uses inexpensive, fresh ingredients that, when served, can be fit for a king. You will notice in looking through these recipes that the same ingredients are used repeatedly, but are put together in different ways. Should you have difficulty obtaining any of the necessary ingredients, please contact us directly.

This book is not merely a cookbook, but an artistic sampling of the scenery and culture of New Mexico. This has been made possible through the beautiful illustrations of Karel Hayes. Not only does Karel's artwork bring the pages to life, but it was her continual encouragement and support--as well as frequent taste testings--that brought THE BROWN ADOBE, Inc. from dream to reality. Karel's watercolor paintings and pen and ink drawings have been exhibited in Philadelphia, New York City, Cincinnati, Maine and other places around the country, including Taos, New Mexico. Her drawings have appeared in several magazines, and she has illustrated five other books.

Should any questions arise as you try these recipes, please contact us. Your suggestions and comments are most welcome!

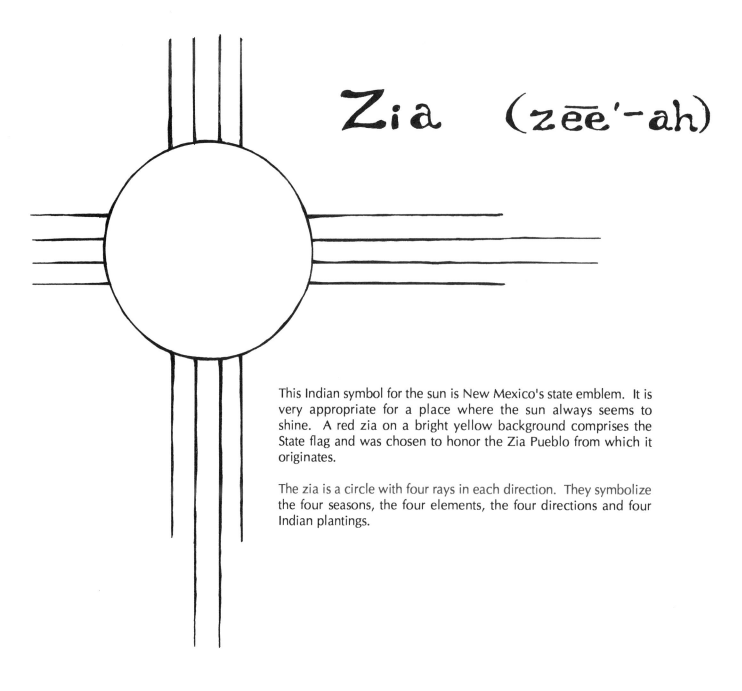

Zia (zēē'-ah)

This Indian symbol for the sun is New Mexico's state emblem. It is very appropriate for a place where the sun always seems to shine. A red zia on a bright yellow background comprises the State flag and was chosen to honor the Zia Pueblo from which it originates.

The zia is a circle with four rays in each direction. They symbolize the four seasons, the four elements, the four directions and four Indian plantings.

Some Like It Hot...and others don't

You can enjoy New Mexican cooking even if you do not like very spicy-hot foods, because <u>you</u> control the heat by selecting the desired temperature of the green chiles and ground red chile. (See "About Chiles" for more information.) In fact, these dishes are so tasty that it is a shame to make them <u>too</u> hot, since it tends to mask the flavor.

New Mexican red and green chiles vary from mild to extra-hot, depending upon how they are cultivated and where they are grown. One factor which affects the temperature is how near to water the chiles are grown or whether there was a drought during the growing season. The drier the soil, the hotter the chile. For reasons no one has been able to document, New Mexican chiles are considered to be the absolute best available. Therefore, it is important that you use only 100% pure New Mexico chile whenever possible.

Because New Mexicans have ready access to even very hot chiles, they don't often use jalapeno peppers. The taste difference between jalapenos and chiles is two-fold:

1. Jalapenos (hal-a-pay'-nyoz) have no real flavor and are all heat, while chiles are very flavorful and can range from mild to scorching.

2. Jalapenos give off an instant hot bite the moment the pepper touches the mouth. A recipe made with hot chiles may not taste hot upon the first bite or two--but it will catch up with you a moment later!

For the above reasons, jalapeno peppers are never specified in these recipes. That, of course, doesn't mean you can't use them. If you like your food so hot your eyes water, go ahead and add jalapenos--but don't say I didn't warn you!!

About Chiles

Although they are considered a vegetable, chiles are classified botanically in the fruit family. And what a great fruit it is! Not necessarily hot, but extremely flavorful, chiles are a staple ingredient of nearly every New Mexican meal. And for good reason--they are delicious! Chiles are also good for us, as they contain more vitamin C than nearly any other fruit or vegetable.

Should you ever see the combined words "chili pepper", you will know you have not found New Mexico green chiles. The first clue is in the spelling of the word. New Mexicans prefer to spell "chile" with one "i" and a final "e". The second clue is the addition of the word "pepper," which New Mexicans do not tack onto their precious green chiles.

Until 1955, the only available chiles were extremely hot. Fortunately, at that time, the late Dr. Roy Nakayama of New Mexico State University cultivated New Mexico #6, a very mild and flavorful chile. Since that time, an entire scale of green chiles has been developed, ranging from the mild Anaheim to a very scorching Bahamian. The green chile harvest begins in late July, when the outermost chiles are picked from the plants.

Buying Green Chiles

Many supermarkets have sections where you can purchase hispanic and other specialty items, including canned green chiles. Unless you are familiar enough with fresh green chiles to know what you are buying, I suggest you stick with the canned variety. As mentioned above, if you find "chili peppers," you can be pretty certain they are not the right thing.

Since green chiles generally come in four-ounce cans, all the recipes herein are written to specify the number of cans needed. Total required ounces are also specified. It is more difficult to find whole green chiles, and those in small cans are often too split to make good chiles rellenos. Let us know if you have difficulty finding any of the ingredients you need to make these recipes.

About Red Chile

In New Mexico, it is rare to find a home without at least one ristra ($\overline{ree}$'-strah), a string of red chiles like those illustrated here. These beautiful red strands give an accent of color to the adobe homes in the early fall and a continuous supply of red chile to the New Mexican cook throughout the year. Red chile is actually green chile which has been allowed to ripen before harvest.

Unfortunately, if you live in an area with more humidity than the American Southwest, you won't be able to have your chiles this way. We found out the hard way, when in only days, our ristra was teaming with fruit flies and growing mold! The best alternative is to buy it already ground, with seeds removed.

Pure ground New Mexico red chile is not the same thing as what is called "chili powder" in the market. Read the label, and you will see several other ingredients have been added to the product. You also don't know whether it is <u>New Mexico</u> red chile, and since we know that is by far the most flavorful, why go through all the work and settle for less flavor? These dishes will be delicious if the right red chile is used. Pure ground New Mexico red chile is available in several temperatures, ranging from mild to extra-hot.

About Tortillas

Fortunately, both corn and flour tortillas are available in many markets. They are often located in the dairy section. You might also find canned tortillas, which we would not recommend unless there is no alternative.

Even in New Mexico, most people do not make tortillas, as they can be readily purchased. However, in case you do not have easy access to them or would like to try to make them, a recipe for flour tortillas has been provided. We have not included one for corn tortillas because they are difficult to make well, and they require masa harina. If you can locate this ingredient, it is likely you will be able to find ready-made corn tortillas.

In New Mexico, blue corn tortillas are popular. These are tortillas made from the blue corn of the Pueblo Indians and are a unique blue-gray color. (This is the type of corn, known as Indian corn, you sometimes see hanging on doors in autumn.) The yield per acre of this corn is far less than that of yellow corn and, therefore, it is quite rare, costly and not widespread outside the Southwest. The blue corn produces a nutty flavor and should be tried if you ever have the opportunity.

Flour tortillas are used as bread by New Mexicans and to make dishes such as burritos. Corn tortillas are often fried and then assembled into enchiladas, tacos or other dishes.

TO FRY CORN TORTILLAS: In a small heavy skillet, place about 1-1/2 cups corn or vegetable oil. Heat oil until very hot (400°F). The tortillas must be <u>dry</u> before they are placed in the oil to avoid spitting. If they are wet or damp, pat with paper towels before lowering (with tongs) into the hot oil. Cook, one at a time, until very crisp (about 1 minute), pressing the tortilla into the oil with the tongs. Remove from oil, allowing excess to drip off, and place in brown grocery bag (or on paper towels) to drain. If your tortillas turn out greasy rather than crisp and dry, either your oil was not hot enough, or you did not cook them long enough. If you plan to make these often, the used oil may be cooled, placed in a jar and saved in the cupboard for the next time you fry tortillas.

Starters

Chile Con Queso (chi-lēē kon kāy´-sō)

This is a warm cheese dip that always draws rave reviews and is very easy to prepare. Serve in a chafing dish to keep it warm, and accompany with tostadas (the New Mexican name for tortilla chips) for dipping.

Preparation and cooking time: 15 minutes
Serve immediately in chafing dish or fondue pot

Makes about 4 cups:
> *1 small onion, finely chopped*
> *1 small clove garlic, minced*
> *1 tablespoon butter*
> *2 cans (8 ounces) green chiles, choppped*
> *1 tablespoon pure ground New Mexico red chile*
> *1/2 pound (regular flavor) Velveeta cheese, cubed**
> *1/2 pound Monterey Jack cheese, grated**
> *1 bag tostadas*

Place top of double boiler directly on burner and melt butter. Add onions and garlic, and cook until softened. Add green chiles and heat through. Stir in red chile. Place pot over hot water and add Velveeta and Jack cheeses.* Stir occasionally until melted and the mixture is hot. This dip must be kept warm while serving, so place in chafing dish with lighted sterno or other heating element. Serve with tostadas.

*If this must be made more than an hour in advance of serving, it is recommended that you use 1 pound of Velveeta and omit the Jack cheese to prevent separation.

VARIATIONS: 1. Add 1 small, ripe tomato, finely chopped, just before serving.
2. For extra flavor, add 2 tablespoons THE BROWN ADOBE Sensational Salsa along with the green chiles.

Guacamole (hwa-ka-mō-lēe)

Don't pronounce the "G" in the name of this garden fresh concoction of mashed avocado, tomatoes and seasonings. A great hors d'oeuvre served with tostadas, this can also be used to garnish entrees such as chalupas or enchiladas, on nachos, or as a salad when served on a bed of lettuce.

Preparation time: 10 minutes (2 minutes for "Quick and Easy")
Prepare at last minute or no more than one hour before serving

To serve 4-6:
>   2 _very ripe_ avocados, chopped
>   1 small ripe tomato, finely chopped
>   1 tiny clove garlic, minced
>   1 tablespoon onion, very finely chopped
>   1/2 can (2 ounces) green chiles, chopped
>   1 teaspoon salt
>   1 teaspoon fresh lemon juice

Mix all of the above ingredients together and mash with a fork or potato masher until well blended. For a more interesting texture and better flavor, do not puree but leave slightly chunky. The taste of your guacamole will depend largely upon the flavor of the avocado used. Those with hard, bumpy, dark skins are most flavorful. Only very ripe avocados will do! If you must prepare this more than a few minutes before serving, place the pit from the avocado into the dip, cover loosely with plastic wrap and put in the refrigerator. This will prevent the guacamole from turning brown. Remove the pit before serving.

"QUICK AND EASY" VERSION:

>   1 very ripe avocado, chopped
>   2 tablespoons THE BROWN ADOBE Sensational Salsa

Combine the above ingredients in a bowl, and mash with a fork or potato masher.
Serve with tostadas, and accept the compliments gracefully
as though it took _hours_ to prepare!

Bean Dip

This hors d'oeuvre is not only delicious and easy to make, but is loaded with protein as well. If you serve this with cold beer on Super Bowl Sunday, be prepared to make another batch!

Preparation time: 5 minutes
Cooking time: 3 minutes in microwave or 10 minutes on stove, then
        2 minutes under preheated broiler

To serve 6-8:
        2 cups refried beans (canned, or recipe on p.50)
        1/2 cup (or more to taste) THE BROWN ADOBE Sensational Salsa
        2 ounces sharp orange Cheddar cheese, grated
        2 ounces Monterey Jack cheese, grated
        1 bag tostadas

Heat beans, add Sensational Salsa and mix well. Top with grated cheeses, and place under broiler until melted and bubbly. Serve with tostadas (the New Mexican name for tortilla chips).

Sensational Nachos

Everyone loves nachos! Crispy tostadas can be topped with just about anything--or almost everything, as in this recipe. These individual nachos can be a meal in themselves and, in fact, can easily be made into Chalupas (cha-loo'-pahz), a New Mexican entree.

To make chalupas, follow this recipe, but <u>do not</u> cut the tortillas before frying. Top the whole fried tortilla with all the fixin's and serve one or two per person. Pick up to eat, as you would tacos.

Preparation time: 15 minutes
Broiling time: 1 minute

To serve 4-8 (makes 32 individual nachos or 8 chalupas):
> *2 cups refried beans (canned or recipe on p.50)*
> *1 large <u>very ripe</u> avocado*
> *8 corn tortillas (quartered for nachos, whole for chalupas)*
> *Oil for frying tortillas (about 1-1/2 cups)*
> *1-1/2 cups THE BROWN ADOBE Sensational Salsa*
> *1/4 pound sharp orange Cheddar cheese, grated*
> *1/4 pound Monterey Jack cheese, grated*
> *1 cup sour cream*
> *8 large black olives, pitted*

Preheat broiler. Heat beans. Peel the avocado, and mash it with 1-2 tablespoons Sensational Salsa to make guacamole.

<u>TO MAKE TOSTADAS:</u> Heat the oil in a heavy skillet. When <u>very hot</u> (400° F), add the quartered tortillas, a few at a time, and fry until crisp (about 1 minute). (<u>Do not</u> cut tortillas if making chalupas.) Remove with slotted spoon and drain on paper towels or in brown bag.

Arrange tostadas on an ovenproof serving platter or cookie sheet and spread each chip with about 1 tablespoon of the beans, 1 teaspoon salsa and about 1 tablespoon of the combined cheeses. (Quadruple these proportions if making chalupas.) Place under the broiler for <u>1 minute</u>, just until the cheese is barely melted. (If you leave them under the broiler too long, they will get soggy and be very messy to pick up.) Remove from heat, top each with 1 teaspoon guacamole, 1 teaspoon sour cream and 1/4 black olive (again, for chalupas, quadruple these measurements and use one whole olive per chalupa).

Margaritas

Frozen and frothy, this drink adds a festive touch before your New Mexican meal or can be served as a dessert. Be careful, however, as they taste sweet and refreshing, but are extremely potent! Thanks to our friend, Philip Dutton, for passing this treat along to us.

To make 6 drinks:

12 ounces Tequila
6 ounces Triple Sec
6 ounces frozen limeade concentrate
Ice cubes
1 lime, cut into 6 wedges
kosher or coarse sea salt

Put the first 3 ingredients in a blender (the limeade container makes a convenient measure). Add ice cubes to fill the blender and grind until it becomes a slush.

To prepare the glasses, rub a slice of lime around the rim, then press the rim into a saucer of the salt. Pour in the slushy drink, and garnish the glass with a wedge of lime.

Soups and Stews

Albondigas Soup

"Albondigas" is Spanish for "meatball". This unusual soup has spicy little meatballs floating in it--and it tastes wonderful! Serve with cheese burritos (p.49), as a refreshingly different dinner.

Preparation time: 45 minutes
Cooking time: 20 minutes (May be made ahead and kept warm)

To serve 4-6:
>3 tablespoons corn oil, divided
>1 large onion, finely chopped (about 1-1/4 cups)
>2 cloves garlic, minced, divided
>1 pound very lean ground beef
>3 tablespoons yellow corn meal
>1/4 teaspoon dried cilantro
>1/2 teaspoon fresh mint leaves, chopped (or 1/4 teaspoon dried)
>1/4 teaspoon ground cumin
>1 egg, slightly beaten
>salt and freshly ground pepper to taste
>1 tablespoon + 1 teaspoon pure ground New Mexico red chile
>3 cups tomatoes, chopped (fresh* or canned)
>1 can (4 ounces) green chiles, chopped
>4 cups chicken broth (canned or homemade)

(Al – bōn´ – dēē – gahz)

In a small saucepan or skillet, heat 1 tablespoon of the oil, and add 1/2 of the garlic and 1/4 cup of the onion. Stir and cook until softened. Meanwhile, in a mixing bowl, place the meat, corn meal, cilantro, mint, cumin, egg, salt, pepper, and 1 teaspoon of the red chile. Add the cooked onions and garlic, combine well and form into small meatballs (about the size of walnuts).

In a large saucepan, heat 1 tablespoon oil, add the remaining garlic and onion, and cook until softened. Add the tomatoes, 1 tablespoon red chile, the green chiles and stir. Add chicken broth, bring to a boil and simmer for about 10 minutes. Meanwhile, heat 1 tablespoon oil in a skillet, and brown the meatballs on all sides. Using a slotted spoon, drain off the grease, add the meatballs to the soup and simmer, covered, for about 20 minutes. Serve in heated bowls with cheese burritos.

*NOTE: If using fresh tomatoes, peel and seed before measuring. See tip on page 22 for easy peeling.

Gazpacho (Gahz-pah´-chō)

While so many New Mexican dishes are terrific on cold winter days, this one is for summer! A terrific way to use your garden-ripe tomatoes, nothing could be tastier--or healthier--on a hot summer day. Make a big batch of this and eat it all week long. It keeps well in the refrigerator for about a week and actually tastes better a day or two after it is prepared. This also makes a nice first course at a summertime dinner party.

Preparation time: 20 minutes
No cooking: Prepare early in day or day ahead

To serve 8:

2 large tomatoes, peeled*
1 medium onion, peeled
1 large cucumber, peeled
1 green pepper, seeded
1 can (4 ounces) green chiles, chopped
1 large can (46 ounces) vegetable juice (such as V-8)
1/4 cup olive oil
1/3 cup red wine vinegar
5 drops Tabasco
1 teaspoon salt
Freshly ground black pepper, to taste
1 clove garlic, minced
Croutons   (optional)

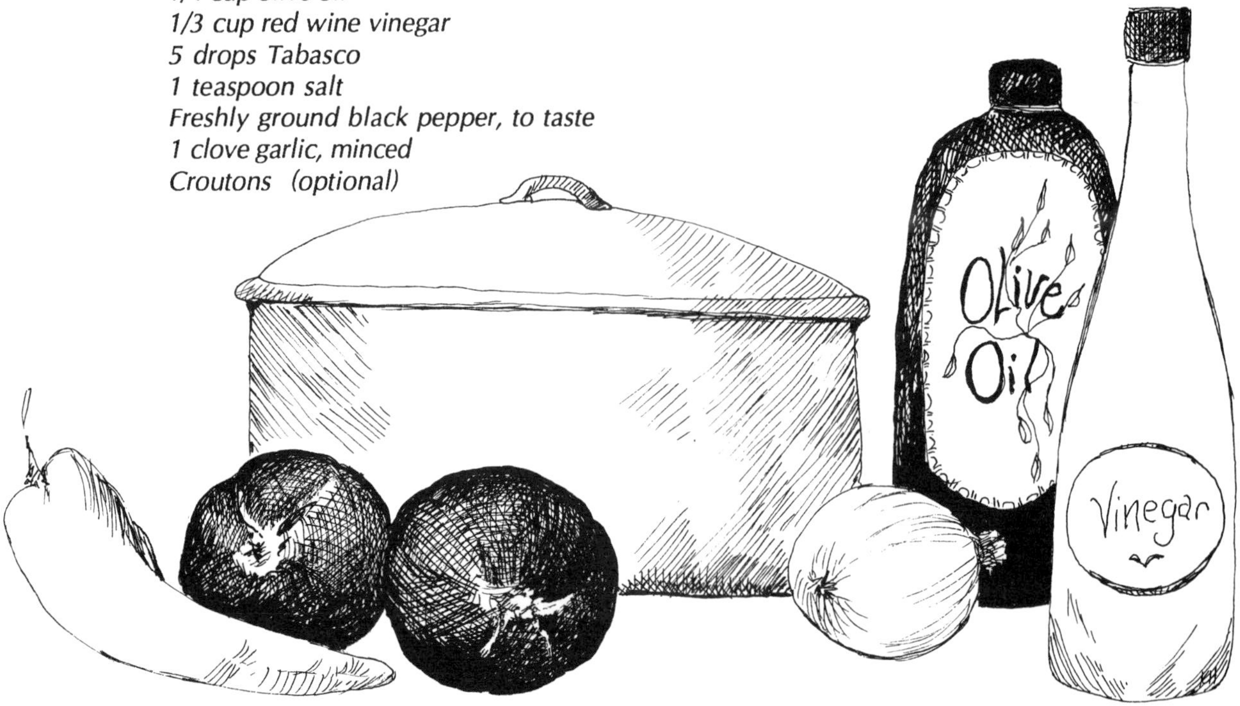

In a food processor fitted with the steel blade, combine 1 tomato, 1/2 onion, 1/2 cucumber, 1/2 green pepper, 1/2 can green chiles and 1 cup vegetable juice. Chop until a puree is formed. Pour this into a large bowl, and add the olive oil, vinegar, Tabasco, salt, pepper and minced garlic. Add the rest of the juice. Finely chop the remaining 1/2 onion and add it to the soup. Dice the remaining tomato, cucumber and green pepper into small bite-sized pieces, and add these along with the rest of the green chiles to the bowl. Stir and refrigerate, covered, for several hours or overnight before serving. As the soup chills, it thickens a bit and the flavors blend together. Serve in small bowls garnished with croutons, if desired.

*TIP: To peel tomatoes easily, dip into boiling water for about 20 seconds, remove with slotted spoon and hold under cold tap water. The skin will come off easily with a paring knife.

Green Chile Stew

This is a wonderful, hearty dish, great when served in winter, but delicious enough to eat anytime. Serve this steaming hot along with cheese burritos (p.49), garlic bread or sopaipillas (p.48). Although a meal in itself, it could be served as a first course for a real feast, or as part of a buffet.

This recipe can easily be modified to feed a crowd or meet a more modest budget. *Some variations include:* 1. Add a can of chopped tomatoes. 2. A popular New Mexican variation is to add 4 or 5 diced, peeled potatoes during the final hour of cooking. 3. Use the same amount of pork, but double the other ingredients. For a huge batch, all 3 above variations could be made! The following version is what we like best:

Preparation time: 20 minutes, total
Cooking time: 4-5 hours

To serve 6-8:

  3 pounds pork roast (shoulder, butt or well-marbled loin)
  2 tablespoons corn (or vegetable) oil
  4 medium onions, chopped
  2 large cloves garlic, minced
  6 cans (24 ounces) green chiles, chopped
  2-1/2 cups beef broth (canned or homemade)
  2 cups water + 1/2 cup to deglaze roasting pan
  1 tablespoon pure ground New Mexico red chile
  1 teaspoon dried oregano
  1/2 teaspoon ground cumin
  Salt and freshly ground black pepper, to taste

About 5 hours before serving: Place pork in pan and roast at 300° F for about 4 hours, until it shreds easily and meat thermometer reads 170° F.

1-2 hours later: Heat oil in large, heavy, covered kettle and gently saute onions until softened. Add garlic, and stir. Add green chiles, beef broth, water and seasonings. Bring to a boil, and then gently simmer, covered, for about 2 hours, stirring occasionally.

  When pork is tender, shred into large bite-sized chunks, and add to the stew. Pour off the drippings from the roasting pan, and deglaze the pan with 1/2 cup water, adding this glaze to the stew.   (If you wish to add potatoes and/or tomatoes, as noted above, do so now.) Simmer for another hour or so.

John Brown's Chili

New Mexicans prefer to spell the chile pepper with an "e," but the stew is spelled with a final "i". The best chili I've ever tasted, this has evolved from an old family recipe. There are no tomatoes in it, and you control the heat by the type of chile powder you use. Unless you like your chili _very_ spicy, I recommend you use a combination of mild and medium hot red chile.

This chili is best prepared in a pressure cooker, as it makes the beans most tender in the least amount of cooking time. However, if you don't have this type of pot, don't worry--it is just as good when made in a regular pot, but requires more cooking time. Directions are included for both methods. This can be made in great quantities, as it keeps well in the freezer and is a wonderful way to get through the cold winter months. Serve with cheese burritos (p.49) or sopaipillas (p.48).

The day before serving: Soak beans
Preparation time: 20 minutes
Cooking time: 4 hours (pressure cooker), or 7 hours (kettle)

To serve 6-8:
> _1 pound dried pinto beans, soaked overnight_
> _2 medium onions, finely chopped_
> _3 cloves garlic, minced_
> _4 cups beef broth (canned or homemade)_
> _3 cups water_
> _2 tablespoons corn (or vegetable) oil_
> _1-1/2 pounds sirloin or chuck, cubed_
> _3 cans (12 ounces) green chiles, chopped_
> _2 teaspoons dried oregano_
> _1 teaspoon ground cumin_
> _6 tablespoons pure ground New Mexico red chile_
> _salt, to taste_

<u>THE DAY BEFORE SERVING</u>: Rinse and pick over beans. Cover with water at least 2 inches over the beans and soak overnight.

TO PREPARE IN PRESSURE COOKER: Drain and rinse beans, place in pressure cooker and cover with 3 cups of the broth and 2 cups water. Add 1 of the onions, 1 clove of garlic, and 1/2 of the oregano, cumin and red chile. Stir, cover and bring to steam. After the pressure cooker begins to "perk," cook beans for 45 minutes.

Meanwhile, place beef in food processor, and pulse <u>slightly</u> until just shredded. (If you do not have a food processor, you may either cut the beef into small bite-sized pieces or use ground beef.) In a large, heavy pot, heat oil and brown the meat. Add the remaining onion and garlic, and cook until soft. Add the green chiles, the remaining 1 cup of water, 1 cup of broth, and the other half of the oregano, cumin and red chile. Add the bean mixture when done.   Lower heat and gently simmer, covered, for about 2 hours, stirring occasionally. Uncover for the next hour or so to allow to thicken. Salt to taste.

TO PREPARE IN KETTLE: Drain and rinse beans. Place the meat in a food processor and pulse until just <u>slightly</u> shredded. (If you do not have a food processor, you may either cut the meat into small bite-sized pieces or use ground beef.) In a large, heavy covered pot, heat oil and brown the meat. Add onions and garlic, and cook until soft. Add green chiles, beans, broth, water and spices. Bring to boil and gently simmer, covered, for about 7 hours, stirring occasionally, until beans are tender. Add a little more water if chili gets too thick. If too watery, uncover for the final hour of cooking. Add salt to taste.

Posole (Pa-sō'-lee)

Made from a corn-like grain bearing the same name, this is a traditional feast day dish of the Pueblo Indians. A meal in itself, this hearty dish is delicious alone or served with cheese burritos (p.49) or garlic bread. We make this every New Year's and several times during the year. If you like unusual dishes, we recommend you give this a try. You really need a pressure cooker for this recipe, as the dried posole takes quite awhile to soften, and fresh posole is difficult to obtain in most parts of the country. (Posole is similar to hominy, but not exactly. We do not recommend the substitution.) If you cannot locate posole, you may order some directly from THE BROWN ADOBE, Inc.

Day before serving: Soak posole overnight in water
Preparation time: 10 minutes
Cooking time: About 4 hours. May be made ahead or frozen

To serve 6-8:

> 12 ounces dried posole
> 3 pound pork roast (shoulder, butt or well-marbled loin)
> 6 cups water + 1/2 cup to deglaze pan
> 1 large onion, finely chopped
> 2 cloves garlic, minced
> 1 teaspoon salt
> 1 tablespoon oregano, plus extra for topping
> 3 tablespoons pure ground New Mexico red chile
> 2 cans (8 ounces) green chiles, chopped
> 1-1/4 cups chicken broth (canned or homemade)
> 1 lime, cut into wedges (1 per serving)

THE DAY BEFORE SERVING: Cover posole with a large quantity of water. Soak overnight.

AT LEAST 4 HOURS BEFORE SERVING: Heat oven to 300° F. Place pork in a roasting pan just large enough to hold it, and roast for about 3 hours, until meat thermometer reads 170° F and pork is tender. Meanwhile, drain and rinse posole. Place posole in pressure cooker with 6 cups water, onion, garlic, salt, oregano and red chile. Bring to steam and gently "perk" for 1-1/2 hours.

Let off steam, open cooker and add green chiles and chicken broth to the posole. Simmer this mixture until the pork is done. Remove pork from oven, shred it into large bite-sized pieces and add to the posole. Pour off the drippings from the roasting pan, and deglaze pan with 1/2 cup water. Add this glaze to the posole and simmer for another hour. (The longer it simmers, the better. Stir occasionally, and add one or two more cups of water if too much liquid cooks out.) Ladle into soup bowls, and sprinkle each bowl of the stew with about 1/4 teaspoon oregano and garnish with a wedge of lime. Squeeze the lime over the posole and enjoy!

TAOS PUEBLO

Pueblo Indians

Some of the greatest influences upon the State of New Mexico in food, art and culture come from the Pueblo Indians. These peoples are not nomadic, but live in organized villages--or pueblos--primarily located along the Rio Grande River. There are many tribes within the State, each with its own customs and government.

The Taos (pronounced to rhyme with "house") Pueblo, illustrated here and on the previous two pages, is very picturesque and unique in its stacked architecture. It is the northernmost of the nineteen pueblos located in New Mexico.

Hearty Entrees

Huevos Rancheros
(hwāy'-vōz ran-chay'-rōz)

This dish, "Ranch-style eggs," is one of the best ways to start the day. It has become the favorite Sunday breakfast at our home. Most likely, your guests will be well satisfied, and you won't need to serve lunch!

Preparation time: 20 minutes
Broiling time: 1-2 minutes. Serve immediately

To serve 6:

12 slices bacon, sausages or other breakfast meat (optional)
6 large flour tortillas
12 eggs
2 cups refried beans (canned or see recipe p.50)
2 cups THE BROWN ADOBE Sensational Salsa
1/4 pound sharp orange Cheddar cheese, grated
1/4 pound Monterey Jack cheese, grated

Preheat broiler. Prepare bacon or other meat as you would normally and keep warm. Heat beans in saucepan or microwave. Heat tortillas for a few seconds in a microwave or in a heavy skillet. (You just want to warm and soften them, NOT make them crisp.) Make eggs according to preference--fried or scrambled.

On each ovenproof* serving plate, place a flour tortilla, spread with 1/3 cup of warm beans and top with 2 cooked eggs. Cover with 1/3 cup Sensational Salsa and the two grated cheeses. Place under preheated broiler until cheese is melted and bubbly. Place meat on the side, if desired, and serve.

*If you don't have ovenproof plates, these may be placed on a cookie sheet to be broiled and then carefully transferred onto serving plates.

Breakfast Burritos

If you don't have the time or appetite for Huevos Rancheros, but want a different, delicious start to your day, try this recipe invented by my son, Daniel, when he was five years old. Not only is it quick and easy to make, but it can be eaten on the run while racing to catch the train or school bus!

Preparation and cooking time: 5-10 minutes

To serve 1:
- *2 slices bacon (optional)*
- *1 teaspoon butter or bacon drippings*
- *1 flour tortilla*
- *1 egg*
- *1 tablespoon THE BROWN ADOBE Sensational Salsa*
- *2 tablespoon grated cheese (Cheddar or Monterey Jack)*

Prepare bacon in skillet or microwave. Heat skillet with butter or drippings. Beat egg and place on skillet. While the egg is cooking, lay cheese and salsa in the middle of it and flip over as you would an omelet. When cheese is melted, place "omelet" down the center of the tortilla, and fold burrito-style (see illustration on page 49, if necessary). If this will be eaten on the run, fold a paper towel or napkin around the bottom half for easy cleanup.

Chiles Rellenos

"Relleno" means "stuffing," and in this recipe, whole green chiles are stuffed with cheese, coated with a light corn batter and deep fried until golden. They are easy to prepare, yet very exotic and delicious. Depending upon the chiles used, this dish can be mild to quite hot. Most canned green chiles available in parts outside the southwestern U.S. are quite mild, so this dish can even be enjoyed by those who have not yet developed a taste for very hot foods. Accompaniments for this include frijoles (p.50), guacamole (p.15) and sopaipillas (p.48).

Preparation time: 30 minutes
Cooking time: 20 minutes. Serve immediately

To serve 6:

> *1 jar THE BROWN ADOBE Sensational Salsa*
> *(or, Green Chile Sauce, p.52)*
> *12 whole green chiles (4 or 5 cans)**
> *1/2 pound sharp Cheddar cheese, cut into strips to fit chiles*
> *1 cup flour, plus extra for dusting chiles*
> *1 teaspoon baking powder*
> *1/2 teaspoon salt*
> *3/4 cup yellow cornmeal*
> *2 eggs*
> *1 cup milk*
> *Oil for deep frying*

Heat the salsa in a saucepan, and keep warm while you prepare the Chiles Rellenos. This makes a perfect sauce to spoon over them when serving. Or, if you prefer, prepare Green Chile Sauce (p.52) instead.

(chil´-ēē rāy-yāy´-nōz)

<u>Make the corn batter:</u> Sift together 1 cup of the flour, baking powder and salt. Add the cornmeal. Beat eggs, mix with milk and stir into dry mixture until smooth.

Carefully pick over the green chiles to be certain they are not split open. (If they are, you can "patch" them by carefully inserting a piece of another chile within the split one. If they are <u>too</u> badly split, reserve them for another use.) Gently stuff each chile with a strip of Cheddar cheese, and pat dry with a paper towel. Dust lightly with flour. Roll the stuffed chile in corn batter and drop into <u>very</u> hot corn oil. (If the oil is not hot enough, the Chile Relleno will be greasy. Test the oil first by dropping a tablespoon of the batter into it. If a doughnut is immediately formed, the oil is hot enough.) When golden brown, remove the chiles rellenos from the oil and drain on paper towels. To serve, arrange 2 chiles rellenos on each plate, and spoon some of the warm salsa or Green Chile Sauce over them.

*It is a good idea to buy more cans of whole green chiles than you think you will need, as you may find some are too badly split to be used for this purpose. Reserve these for another use.

White Sands National Monument

Tacos

If the only tacos you have made are those that come in a box, you are in for a treat when you try this. These make a terrific family dinner as they not only are fun to eat, but also contain all four food groups in one handy shell. One secret to great tacos is in the shell. With only a little more work and time, you can prepare your own shells rather than using the prepackaged variety, which will make a world of difference in the finished product.

We make these so often, we developed THE BROWN ADOBE Spice Mix to make preparation even easier. Unlike other "taco mix," this contains only natural ingredients in the correct proportions to make taco night extra easy for the cook. The following recipe includes directions for making tacos from scratch, as well as with the mix.

Preparation and cooking time: 30 minutes (shells may be prepared hours ahead, if desired)
Broiling time: 1-2 minutes

To serve 4-6 (makes 12 tacos):
1 pound beef, shredded or ground
1 small onion, finely chopped
1 clove garlic, minced
1 can (4 ounces) green chiles, chopped
1 tablespoon pure ground New Mexico red chile
1 teaspoon oregano
1/2 teaspoon salt
1/2 teaspoon ground cumin
Freshly ground black pepper, to taste
1/8 teaspoon dried cilantro (optional)
12 corn tortillas
Oil for frying tortillas (about 1-1/2 cups)
1/4 pound sharp orange Cheddar cheese, grated
1/4 pound Monterey Jack cheese, grated
THE BROWN ADOBE Sensational Salsa
2 tomatoes, diced
6 lettuce leaves, chopped

Heat skillet and brown beef. Drain off all grease and add onion, green chile and garlic. (Omit garlic if using THE BROWN ADOBE Spice Mix.) Add the dried spices (or, 1-1/2 tablespoons Spice Mix). Stir and simmer, covered, on lowest heat while you prepare taco shells.

To Prepare Taco Shells: In a 10-inch heavy skillet, heat oil until it is <u>very hot</u> (about 400°F). Using tongs, gently lower a dry corn tortilla into the hot oil. After 5-10 seconds, fold the tortilla in half and hold in taco shell shape until one side is crisp (about 20 seconds). With the tongs, hold the shell <u>open</u> as it cooks, so there will be room to stuff it without breaking. Turn and fry until crisp on the other side. Remove from oil and allow excess oil to drip off, then place in brown grocery bag to drain. (If your shells are greasy rather than dry and very crisp, either the oil was not hot enough, or you did not cook them long enough.) It takes about 15 minutes to make a dozen shells. If they do not come out perfectly, do not despair. It takes a little practice to get the knack, but you will be glad you did.

When you are ready to eat, preheat broiler. Fill each shell with approximately 1/3 cup of the meat and 2-3 tablespoons of the combined cheeses. Place under broiler for 1-2 minutes to melt the cheese. Serve along with THE BROWN ADOBE Sensational Salsa, lettuce and tomatoes, allowing diners to add toppings as desired.

<u>VARIATION</u>: Use your imagination to fill the taco shells. Try this: Fill shells with cooked shredded chicken, THE BROWN ADOBE Sensational Salsa, guacamole (recipe p.15), sour cream, lettuce, tomato and black olives.

Stacked Enchiladas with Red Chile

Most people think of enchiladas as cheese, meat, and/or beans <u>rolled</u> up in corn tortillas, as described on page 42. This is one way to serve them, but an easy, delicious and very New Mexican way to prepare enchiladas is <u>stacked</u>. The difference is in the preparation and assembly of the tortillas. In New Mexico, blue corn tortillas are often used and should be tried if you can find them. Don't let the apparent length of this recipe frighten you off! It is easy to prepare, tastes terrific, and will certainly impress your guests.

While we usually use beef, this is also terrific with ground or shredded chicken or turkey. We prefer to grind the meat <u>only slightly</u> in a food processor. If you prefer, you may purchase ready ground meat.

Placing a fried egg on top is authentically New Mexican. If you prefer a different touch, top the enchilada stack with a dollop of sour cream, and surround it with chopped black olives, as well as lettuce and tomato. This dish is not only delicious, but is beautiful when served!

Preparation time: 30 minutes. The Caribe may be made in advance and kept warm, or it may be made ahead and frozen. The tortillas may be fried a few hours in advance.
Broiling time: 1-2 minutes

To Serve 6:
> *Caribe (recipe on page 51)*
> *2 pounds meat (beef, chicken or turkey), slightly ground*
> *1 large onion, finely chopped*
> *2 cloves garlic, minced*
> *2 cans (8 ounces) green chiles, chopped*
> *4 teaspoons dried oregano*
> *1 teaspoon ground cumin*
> *1/2 teaspoon salt*
> *Freshly ground black pepper, to taste*
> *18 corn tortillas*
> *Oil for frying tortillas, about 1-1/2 cups*
> *3/4 pound sharp orange Cheddar cheese, grated*
> *3/4 pound Monterey Jack cheese, grated*
> *3 tomatoes, chopped*
> *12 lettuce leaves, chopped*
> *1 can ripe olives, chopped (optional)*
> *1 pint sour cream (optional)*
> *6 eggs, fried (over easy) at the last minute (optional)*

In a medium saucepan, make Caribe and keep warm. In a skillet, brown meat well and drain off all grease. Add onions and garlic and cook until softened. Add green chile and remaining spices. Ladle about 1 cup of Caribe into meat. Cover and keep warm.

PREPARE TORTILLAS: In a heavy skillet, heat the oil until very hot (about 400°F). Using tongs, slide a dry corn tortilla into the oil, and fry each for about 1 minute. Remove from oil, allowing excess to drip off, and place in brown paper bag to drain.

ASSEMBLE ENCHILADAS: Preheat broiler. Holding a tortilla with tongs, dip it into the Caribe until it is well coated. Place on ovenproof plate which has a lip to hold the sauce. Spoon about 1/4 cup of the meat onto this tortilla, add a handful of the two cheeses and more Caribe. Do this on each of 6 dinner plates. Repeat this procedure for a second layer. Top each with a third well-sauced tortilla, and add a generous helping of sauce and cheese. Set under broiler until the cheese melts (about 1-2 minutes). Surround each stack with a "wreath" of lettuce and tomato, and top with an egg (fried, over easy) or sour cream and chopped black olives.

Stacked Enchiladas with Chicken and Green Chiles

Delicious and easy to prepare, this is one of my favorite dishes. It can be made several hours before serving, with only last minute assembly needed. A meal in itself, it needs no accompaniments. Make sure you set out spoons, as well as knives and forks, so you don't waste a drop of this flavorful sauce!

Preparation time: 35 minutes
Cooking time: Minimum 30 minutes
Broiling time: 1-2 minutes

To serve 4:
*1 pound boneless chicken breasts,
    cooked and cut into bite-sized pieces
1 tablespoon butter
1 large onion, finely chopped
2 cloves garlic, minced
3 cans (12 ounces) green chiles, chopped
2 cans condensed cream of chicken soup
2-1/2 cups chicken broth (canned or homemade)
2 teaspoons dried oregano
1/2 teaspoon ground cumin
4 teaspoons pure ground New Mexico red chile
12 corn tortillas
Oil for frying tortillas (about 1-1/2 cups)
1/2 pound sharp orange Cheddar cheese, grated
1/2 pound Monterey Jack cheese, grated
2 tomatoes, chopped
8 lettuce leaves, chopped*

Cook and cut up chicken. Meanwhile, heat butter in large saucepan. Add onions and garlic, and cook until softened. Stir in green chiles, soup, broth, spices and cooked chicken. Simmer over very low heat for at least 30 minutes, stirring occasionally, to allow the flavors to mingle.

While this cooks, pour oil into a heavy skillet and heat until <u>very hot</u> (about 400˚ F). Using tongs, slide one dry corn tortilla into the hot oil, and cook for about 1 minute, turning once. Remove from oil, allowing excess to drip off, then place in a brown paper bag to drain. *Up to this point, the meal may be prepared a couple of hours ahead of serving.*

<u>TO ASSEMBLE ENCHILADAS</u>: Preheat broiler. Place one tortilla on each of 4 individual ovenproof plates with a lip on the rim to hold the sauce. Cover each tortilla with approximately 1/2 cup of the chicken sauce and combined cheeses. Top each with another tortilla and continue this process two more times. End with remaining sauce and grated cheese. Place under broiler for 1-2 minutes until cheese is melted. Make a "wreath" around each tortilla stack with the chopped lettuce and tomato.

Rolled Enchiladas

The stacked enchiladas described in this book are unique to New Mexico. The rolled version is more widespread. Authentic enchiladas are stuffed only with cheese, but they also can be stuffed with beef, chicken, beans, sour cream or a combination of these ingredients. The difference between stacked and rolled enchiladas is in the assembly. For rolled enchiladas, it is not necessary to pre-fry the tortillas as you would for the stacked version. This type may also be prepared in a baking pan and, therefore, be more easily served in a buffet or along with several other dishes, such as tacos or burritos.

Our favorite rolled version is chock full of meat and cheese, and is smothered with Caribe and more cheese. Experiment until you find your favorite combination!

Preparation time: 30 minutes
Baking time: 15-20 minutes at 350 ° F

To serve 6:

Caribe (recipe on page 51)
1 pound beef, ground or shredded slightly in food processor
   (or, 1 pound chicken, cooked and shredded)
1 medium onion, finely chopped
1 large clove garlic, minced
1 can (4 ounces) green chiles, chopped
1 teaspoon oregano
1/2 teaspoon cumin
salt and pepper, to taste
1/2 pound sharp orange Cheddar cheese, grated
1/2 pound Monterey Jack cheese, grated
12 corn tortillas

Preheat oven to 350° F. Make Caribe and keep warm. If using beef, brown meat in a skillet and drain off all grease. (If using chicken, add meat _after_ cooking the onions and garlic in 1 tablespoon oil.) Add onions and garlic, and cook until softened. Add green chiles, oregano, cumin, salt and pepper, and 1/2 cup Caribe. Cover and keep warm on very low heat.

Using tongs, dip a corn tortilla in the Caribe. Place in a 9" x 13" baking pan or in an individual ovenproof serving dish (one dish per guest). Place approximately 1/4 cup meat mixture and 2 tablespoons of the two cheeses down the center of the tortilla. Fold tortilla edges together to form a tube, and arrange seam side down in baking dish. Generously cover with Caribe, and top with the remaining grated cheeses.

Place in 350°F oven for 20-25 minutes until bubbly and cheese is melted. These may be served with refried beans, a salad, guacamole or in combination with another entree such as tacos.

Burritos (bu-ree´-toz)

Burritos are flour tortillas wrapped around a filling of your choice--traditionally beans and/or meat. They can be folded, as on page 49, to be eaten on the go, but are especially delicious when served smothered in either red or green chile sauce. We like to make them with beef, and prefer to serve them in individual dishes to best hold the sauce. Serve with guacamole (p.15), if you wish.

Preparation time: 20 minutes
Broiling time: 2 minutes

To serve 6:

Caribe (p. 51) or Green Chile Sauce (p. 52)
1-1/2 pounds very lean ground beef
1 tablespoon corn (or vegetable) oil
1 medium onion, finely chopped
1 clove garlic, minced
1/2 teaspoon oregano
12 flour tortillas
1/2 pound sharp orange Cheddar cheese, grated
1/2 pound Monterey Jack cheese, grated

Prepare either red (Caribe) or green chile sauce as recipe directs. While this simmers, heat the oil in a skillet and brown the beef. Drain off grease, add the onion and garlic and cook until softened. Add oregano, cover and gently simmer for about 5 minutes.

Place about 1/2 cup of the beef mixture down the center of a flour tortilla, add about 2 tablespoons of the combined cheeses, and fold the two sides together to form a roll. (You do not have to fold up the bottom, as you would for the burritos you pick up to eat.) Arrange 2 burritos on each plate or serving dish, seam side down. Smother in either red or green chile sauce. Top with a generous amount of the combined cheeses, and broil for about 2 minutes until the cheese is bubbly.

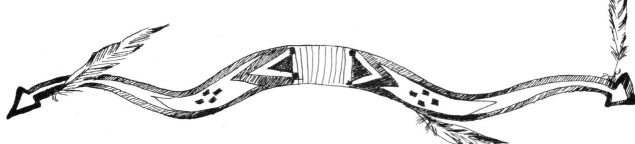

Carne Adovada
(kar'-nāy ah-dō-vah-dah)

Only in New Mexico will you find this wonderful dish of pork, marinated and roasted in a red chile sauce. (The name translates loosely into "marinated meat.") It takes only minutes to prepare and hours to slowly roast in the oven, which makes it great for those dinners where you don't have the time or desire for lots of last-minute preparation.

Carne adovada is delicious served with frijoles (p.50), guacamole (p.15) and sopaipillas (p.48). For a more casual dish or to use leftovers, serve it wrapped up with cheese in a flour tortilla as a carne adovada burrito.

Preparation time: 10 minutes
Cooking time: About 4 hours in 275° F oven, with occasional basting

To serve 6:

3-4 pound pork roast (shoulder, butt or well-marbled loin)
1 large onion
2 large cloves garlic
1-1/4 cups beef broth (canned or homemade)
2 cups water
4 tablespoons pure ground New Mexico red chile
1 teaspoon dried oregano

Place the pork in a roasting pan just slightly larger than needed to hold it. In a food processor or blender, mince the onion and garlic. Add the remaining ingredients, and beat until the consistency of tomato sauce. Pour this over the pork, and bake at 275°F for about 4 hours (a meat thermometer should read 170°F), basting the pork occasionally with the red chile sauce. The sauce will thicken a bit while cooking and may need to be stirred occasionally. If it gets too thick for basting, add a little more water.

To serve, shred the pork into large bite-sized pieces, discarding bones, if any. Stir the pork and red chile sauce together to coat all the meat with the sauce. Serve on heated plate or in tortillas as noted above.

◆　　　◆　　　◆

Kachinas (ka-chēē'-nahz)

The ancient ancestors of the Pueblo Indians were guided by gods called Kachinas. They are represented in the ceremonial dances of the Pueblo peoples, and dolls are made to aid in teaching the children about these spirits.

Missionaries were unsuccessful in eliminating kachinas from Indian religious rites. In many pueblos, Christianity is practiced along with the traditional Indian religion.

Extras

Sopaipillas (sō-pī-pēe-yahz)

Nowhere in the world will you find sopaipillas like those from New Mexico. Golden, light puffs of bread, they are served steaming hot with honey or honey butter. Not only are they delicious, but they act to cool down palates hot from spicy foods. Another New Mexican dish is Stuffed Sopaipillas, in which these puffs of bread are filled with beans or meat (as prepared for burritos on page 44) and smothered with either red or green chile sauce.

Preparation time: 10 minutes, plus 1 hour to rise
Frying time: About 1 minute each. Serve immediately

To make 8-10 sopaipillas:
> *2 cups flour*
> *1 teaspoon baking powder*
> *1 teaspoon sugar*
> *1/2 teaspoon salt*
> *1-1/2 teaspoons lard**
> *1/2 cup warm water*
> *Oil for deep frying (about 2 cups)*
> *4 tablespoons butter, softened*
> *1/4 cup honey*

Sift the dry ingredients together. Thoroughly cut in lard. Stir in water, a little at a time, and knead (for about 5 minutes) until a stiff dough is formed. Cover bowl with a cloth, and allow to rise for about 1 hour in a warm place. Make honey butter by creaming together butter and honey until smooth.

Start heating oil. Roll dough very thin (about 1/8"). Cut into squares or triangles about 3-4 inches on a side. Immerse into very hot oil (about 400° F). Cook just until they puff up and turn golden brown. Serve immediately. To eat, slit open one end and insert some honey butter (or just a little honey).

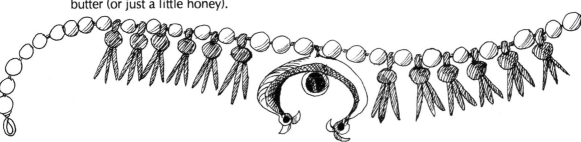

*Lard is authentic and more flavorful, but shortening may be substituted.

Cheese Burritos

These make a nice accompaniment to New Mexican soups and stews. You can also add a little salsa or green chiles to them and serve as a light lunch by themselves--a New Mexican grilled cheese sandwich!

Preparation and cooking time: less than 5 minutes

To make 1 (allow 1 or 2 burritos per person):
1 flour tortilla
3-4 tablespoons grated cheese (we use Cheddar, or a
combination of Cheddar and Monterey Jack)

<u>May be prepared 3 ways:</u>
1. **Microwave:** (This is the best way, as the cheese melts but the tortilla remains soft.) Arrange cheese on tortilla as illustrated, place flat in microwave on high power for about 30 seconds, then fold.

2. **Broiler:** On cookie sheet, lay tortillas flat. Arrange cheese and broil just until cheese is melted, taking care not to overcook tortillas. Fold.

3. **Skillet:** Heat heavy skillet without grease. Place tortilla in pan just until hot, flip over, arrange cheese. Heat about 15 seconds and fold.

<u>TO STUFF AND FOLD TORTILLAS TO MAKE BURRITOS:</u> Arrange cheese (or other stuffing) in the middle of the flour tortilla. Fold up about 1/4 of the bottom. Fold over the left 1/3, then the right 1/3, as shown below. Pick up and eat!

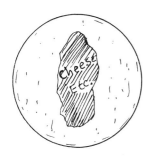  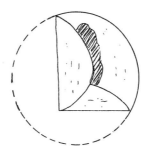 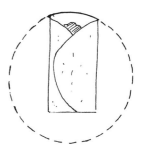

Frijoles Refritos
(free-hō-layz rē-free'-tōz)

"Refried beans" are often served with New Mexican food as a side dish and are very good and filling, as well as high in protein. They are called "refried", since this is how they are often reheated (usually in bacon drippings). Canned refried beans are a convenience and not bad, but nothing compares to a freshly made batch. Whether using canned or freshly prepared beans, the best way to serve them is topped with some Caribe (recipe p.51) or salsa, and melted cheese. Hint: Make a large batch and have Huevos Rancheros (p.32) for the next day's breakfast or Sensational Nachos or Chalupas (p.17) the next evening.

The Day Before: Soak beans in water overnight
Preparation time: 15 minutes
Cooking time: 2 hours (pressure cooker), or 4-6 hours (kettle)

To serve 6-8:
> 1 pound dried pinto beans, soaked overnight
> 5 cups water
> 2 teaspoons salt
> 6 slices bacon, cooked crisp and finely diced*
> 2 tablespoons bacon drippings*
> 1 medium onion, chopped
> 1 large clove garlic, minced

THE DAY BEFORE SERVING: Rinse and pick over beans. Cover with water at least 2 inches over the beans and soak overnight.

THE DAY OF SERVING: Drain and rinse beans. Place all the above ingredients in a pressure cooker or covered kettle, stir well and bring to a boil. **UNDER PRESSURE**, simmer for 1 hour, then simmer partially covered, stirring occasionally, until water is reduced and the sauce is thickened (about 1 more hour). Or, **IN KETTLE**, gently simmer 4-6 hours, covered for at least the first two hours, stirring occasionally and adding boiling water, if beans become too thick before tender. Remove cover for the last hours of cooking, especially if the beans are very watery. They should become the consistency of a thick soup (not like oatmeal, since the beans will thicken even more when mashed). Mash the cooked beans with a potato masher, and serve plain or topped with Caribe (or salsa) and cheese.

*If you have a leftover ham bone, you may use it in place of the bacon and drippings.

Caribe (ka-rēe'-bāy)

Caribe is a red chile sauce which is an essential part of several New Mexican recipes, such as red enchiladas (stacked or rolled) or burritos. It also is delicious when used as a topping on foods such as eggs, beans, etc. Caribe is easy to make and freezes well. We usually make a double batch and freeze the extra portion for another use.

Preparation time: 10 minutes
Cooking time: 15 minutes or longer. May be made up to two days
in advance and refrigerated, or well in advance and frozen

To serve 6 as an enchilada sauce:
4 tablespoons corn oil
6 tablespoons flour
8 tablespoons pure ground New Mexico red chile
2-1/2 cups beef broth (canned or homemade)
2-1/2 cups water
2 large cloves garlic, minced

In a large saucepan, heat oil. Add flour, stirring with whisk until hot and bubbly. Add red chile and whisk until it is mixed with the flour. Slowly, add broth and whisk until all lumps are removed. Add garlic and water and whisk until smooth. Simmer <u>at least</u> 15 minutes. Keep warm until ready to assemble enchiladas.

Organ Mountains

Green Chile Sauce

This sauce is delicious over burritos, stuffed sopaipillas, chiles rellenos or other New Mexican dishes.

Preparation time: 5 minutes. May be made ahead or frozen
Cooking time: 15 minutes or longer

To make about 2-1/2 cups:
> *2 tablespoons corn oil*
> *1 medium onion, finely chopped*
> *1 clove garlic, minced*
> *1 tablespoon cornstarch*
> *1-1/4 cups chicken broth (canned or homemade)*
> *3 cans (12 ounces) green chiles, chopped*
> *1/2 teaspoon baking soda**

In a small heavy saucepan, heat oil and saute onions and garlic until softened. Add the cornstarch and heat through. Add the broth in a stream, stirring constantly until smooth. Add green chiles and bring to a boil. Reduce heat, add the baking soda and stir. (The sauce will foam as the baking soda removes the citric acid from the canned chiles.) Cover and simmer gently for <u>at least</u> 15 minutes to blend the flavors.

*Omit baking soda if using fresh or frozen green chiles. Its purpose is merely to remove the acidity from the canned product, which greatly improves the flavor.

Tortillas (Tor - tēē'-yahz)

If you cannot locate flour tortillas in your market, try this recipe, given to us by Noel Hager of Albuquerque.

Preparation time: 20 minutes, plus 1/2 hour to rest
Cooking time: 2 minutes each

To make about 8 tortillas:
> 2 cups flour
> 2 teaspoons baking powder
> 1/2 teaspoon salt
> 2 tablespoons lard*
> warm water - about 1/2 cup

Sift together the flour, baking powder and salt. Work in the lard with a pastry cutter. Adding just enough water so the dough holds together, knead for about 3 minutes. Cover with a towel, and allow the dough to rest for about 1/2 hour.

Pull off dough to form egg-sized balls, and roll out to form a circle (about 6 inches in diameter). Place the tortillas on a hot griddle or heavy skillet and cook for about 1 minute on each side. They will remain mostly white with little golden brown spots on them. Don't overcook them, or they will be too crisp to fold.

*Lard is the authentic ingredient, works best and is more flavorful, but shortening may be substituted.

Gila Cliff Dwelling

Luminarias (loo-min-ar'-ee-ahz)

At Christmas time in New Mexico, luminarias line adobe roofs and pathways and light up the night. Paper sacks containing sand and a lighted candle, luminarias make a beautiful sight to behold!

This tradition was started on December 12, 1598 at the San Juan Pueblo. On that night, nine luminarias were placed in front of each home--three for the Holy Family, three for the wise men and three for the shepherds. They were lit every night until Christmas.

Sweet Endings

Sweet Endings

Favorite desserts of New Mexico usually include the flavors of cinnamon, chocolate, coffee or anise.

Since we are usually so satisfied (and full!) after one of these dinners, we rarely have dessert. When entertaining, however, you might want to serve your guests a sweet ending, so a few ideas are provided here. In addition to the recipes in this section, you could consider a simple dessert of fresh fruit, ice cream, sherbert or sorbet. Cantaloupe or other tasty melon served with a squeeze of fresh lime is also a refreshing way to end a spicy dinner.

Ice cream layered in parfait glasses with a little Creme de Menthe, Kahlua or Tia Maria is a festive, pretty and tasty ending. Serve with small cups of strong black coffee.

Natillas (nah-tēē´-yahz)

This light custard is a traditional New Mexican dessert. It is excellent served alone with strong black coffee or, if you prefer, garnished with a few slices of seasonal fresh fruit.

Preparation and cooking time: 30 minutes
        Make early in day or day before serving

To serve 4-6:
        2 eggs, separated
        1-1/2 tablespoons flour
        2 cups whole milk
        1/4 cup granulated sugar
        a pinch of salt
        1/4 teaspoon vanilla
        cinnamon for garnish

In a small bowl, beat the egg yolks, flour and 1/2 cup of the milk. Place the remaining 1-1/2 cups milk in a small saucepan, add sugar and salt, and scald over medium heat. Slowly add the egg mixture to the scalded milk, and cook over medium heat, stirring constantly, for about 20 minutes until it becomes a soft custard. Stir in vanilla. Set aside to cool to room temperature.

Beat egg whites until stiff but not dry, then fold into custard. Chill well. To serve, stir and spoon into small dishes or sherbert glasses, and garnish with cinnamon.

57

Bizcochitos (biz-kō-chee´-tōz)

The traditional Christmas cookie of New Mexico, these lightly flavored anise drops melt in your mouth. If you ever get to Albuquerque, make a point to stop by Enchantment Delights, a little cafe in Old Town where Frances Maldonado serves the most delicious bizcochitos. She would not divulge the secret of her recipe, a combination of those from her mother and grandmother. (And we can't blame her!) We are, however, able to provide you with this excellent version, given to us by Susan Hager of Albuquerque.

Preparation time: 20 minutes
Baking time: 7-10 minutes at 350°F

To make about 60 small cookies:
> 1 cup (1/2 pound) lard, softened
> 1-1/2 cups granulated sugar, divided
> 1 teaspoon anise seed
> 1 egg
> 3 cups flour, sifted
> 1-1/2 teaspoons baking powder
> 1/2 teaspoon salt
> 2-3 tablespoons water
> 2 teaspoons cinnamon

In a food processor or mixing bowl, cream lard and 3/4 cup sugar. Add anise. Beat egg and add to mixture. Blend until light and fluffy.

Sift flour with baking powder and add salt. Combine with creamed sugar mixture. Knead in just enough water so dough holds together. Roll 1/2-inch thick and cut into shapes with a 1- or 2-inch cookie cutter. (The traditional shape is a fleur-de-lis.) Bake at 350° F until barely browned, about 7-10 minutes. Thoroughly mix the remaining 3/4 cup sugar with the cinnamon. Roll the cookies while still hot in this sugar mixture, coating generously.

Roadrunner

This refreshing milkshake, <u>for adults only</u>, is named after New Mexico's state bird, often seen running along the roads and amongst the sagebrush. While it is not an "authentic" dish from this state, we combined some of the popular flavors--chocolate and coffee--with Mexican liqueur and the refreshing taste of mint.

To serve 4:
       1 pint chocolate ice cream
       1 pint coffee ice cream
       1 jigger Kahlua brand liqueur
       1 jigger Peppermint Schnapps

Place all ingredients in blender and beat until smooth. Pour into large wine or old fashion glasses. Serve with cookies, such as bizcochitos, for dessert.

Capirotada (kah-pēē-rō-tah-dah)

This delicious bread pudding is also known as sopa (sō'-pah) which, oddly enough, means "soup" in Spanish. In no way soup-like, it makes a very satisfying dessert despite its unusual ingredients. Leftovers, if you are lucky enough to have any, may be reheated in a microwave. Special thanks to Carolyn Pryor and Amy Boule of Albuquerque for giving us this recipe.

Preparation time: 15 minutes. May be made <u>partially</u> ahead
Baking time: 40 minutes at 325 ° F. Serve warm

To serve 8:
>1 (1 pound) loaf good quality white bread
>1 cup raisins
>1/2 pound (about 2 cups) Longhorn cheese, grated
>1/4 pound (1 stick) butter
>3/4 cup granulated sugar
>1 cup water
>1 tablespoon cinnamon
>1 cup heavy cream

Use some of the butter to grease a 9" x 13" pan. Remove crusts from the bread, and cut into 1-inch cubes. Cut the butter into 1/2-inch cubes. Layer half of the bread, raisins, butter and cheese. Repeat, ending with cheese on top. Up to this point, the capirotada can be made ahead and refrigerated until about 1 hour before serving.

<u>One hour before serving</u>: Preheat oven to 325° F. <u>Make syrup</u>: In a small saucepan, combine sugar, water and cinnamon. Stirring constantly, boil until slightly thick (like heavy cream), but not long enough to caramelize. Carefully pour the syrup over the layered bread mixture. Cover with foil and bake for 40 minutes. Serve warm, topped with slightly whipped cream.

The Storyteller

The beautiful pottery of the Pueblo Indians is well known, and fine pieces are collected worldwide. One unique example of this pottery is the Storyteller.

These are whimsical figurines of an adult crawling with children in various moods and positions. The storyteller's mouth is perpetually open, informing the children of life in the pueblos and telling tales of the past. Handmade, the storytellers are dressed in traditional garb and are usually painted in hues of black, red and white. Some of the storytellers are in animal form, as illustrated here.

Index